AIR FRYER COOKBOOK FOR BEGINNERS

The Bible of air fryer cooking. 1500 days of tasty and easy-to-cook recipes. Discover the pleasure of fried food even if you want to be healthy. FULL COLOR EDITION

Margaret Salt

© Copyright 2022 by Margaret Salt- All rights reserved.

This document is geared towards providing exact and reliable information in regards to the topic and issue covered. The publication is sold with the idea that the publisher is not required to render accounting, officially permitted, or otherwise, qualified services. If advice is necessary, legal or professional, a practiced individual in the profession should be ordered.

- From a Declaration of Principles which was accepted and approved equally by a Committee of the American Bar Association and a Committee of Publishers and Associations.

In no way is it legal to reproduce, duplicate, or transmit any part of this document in either electronic means or in printed format. Recording of this publication is strictly prohibited and any storage of this document is not allowed unless with written permission from the publisher. All rights reserved.

The information provided herein is stated to be truthful and consistent, in that any liability, in terms of inattention or otherwise, by any usage or abuse of any policies, processes, or directions contained within is the solitary and utter responsibility of the recipient reader. Under no circumstances will any legal responsibility or blame be held against the publisher for any reparation, damages, or monetary loss due to the information herein, either directly or indirectly.

Respective authors own all copyrights not held by the publisher.

The information herein is offered for informational purposes solely, and is universal as so. The presentation of the information is without contract or any type of guarantee assurance.

The trademarks that are used are without any consent, and the publication of the trademark is without permission or backing by the trademark owner. All trademarks and brands within this book are for clarifying purposes only and are the owned by the owners themselves, not affiliated with this document.

Table of content

INTRODUCTION 5
CHAPTER 1. WHAT IS AN AIR FRYER? 6
    1.1. How Do Air Fryers Function? 6
    1.2. Advantages of air fryers 6
CHAPTER 2. HOW TO USE AN AIR FRYER? 8
    2.1. Which Air Fryer Is the Best? 8
    2.2. How to Wash an Air Fryer Completely 8
CHAPTER 3. GENERAL TIPS FOR AIR FRYING 10
    3.1. Getting Ready to Air-Fry 10
    3.2. While Air Frying the Food 10
    3.3. After Air-Frying 11
CHAPTER 4. FREQUENTLY ASKED QUESTIONS ABOUT AIR FRYER 12
AIR FRYER RECIPES 13
    CHICKEN BREAST 14
    SWEET CHILI CHICKEN BITES 15
    BUFFALO CHICKEN WINGS 17
    HEALTHY CHICKEN AND VEGGIES 18
    SPICY CHICKEN AND BROCCOLI 19
    HEALTHY PORK CHOPS 20
    ITALIAN PORK CHOPS 21
    ASIAN PORK MEATBALLS 22
    YUMMY PORK ROAST 24
    EASY PULLED PORK 25
    JUICY TURKEY BURGERS 26
    HEALTHY TURKEY BREAST 27
    TASTY TURKEY MEATBALLS 28
    TURKEY TENDERLOIN BAKED 29
    HEALTHY TURKEY CROQUETTES 30
    ROAST-STYLE BABY POTATOES 31
    HEALTHY HASH BROWNS 32
    CHEESY BUFFALO CAULIFLOWERS BITES 33
    CRISPY VEGETABLES 34
    STUFFED SWEET POTATOES 35
    AIR FRIED FILET MIGNON 36
    EASY MONGOLIAN BEEF 37
    GARLIC BUTTER STEAKS 39
    STEAK BITES & MUSHROOMS 40
    JUICY ONION SOUP MIX BURGERS 41
    BAKED MAPLE SALMON 43
    AIR FRIED JUMBO SHRIMP 44
    JUICY GARLIC BUTTER SHRIMP 46
    CRAB STUFFED MUSHROOMS 47
    AIR FRIED MAHI MAHI 48

FALAFEL *49*
VEGETARIAN SPRING ROLLS *51*
VEGAN AIR FRIED RAVIOLI *53*
POPCORN TOFU *54*
VEGAN CRUNCH WRAP *55*
BAKED APPLE CHIPS *56*
AIR FRYER TATER TOTS *57*
CANDIED WALNUTS *58*
LOW CARB AIR FRIED ONION RINGS *59*
AIR FRIED MACARONI&CHEESE BALL *60*
AIR FRIED BUTTERNUT SQUASH *61*
ROASTED GARLIC GREEN BEANS *62*
CRISPY AIR FRIED FRENCH FRIES *63*
2-INGREDIENT DOUGH BAGELS *64*
CRISPY POTATO WEDGES *65*
EASY BLUEBERRY MUFFIN BITES *66*
HONEY GLAZED PEARS *67*
NUTELLA FRENCH TOAST ROLL-UPS *68*
QUICK BROWNIES *69*
PLAIN CAKE *70*

4 WEEKS MEAL PLAN **71**

CONCLUSION **72**

Introduction

Many of us who cook at home regularly is hunting for things that will make cooking faster, easier, or more flavorful or all of the above. Consequently, it is no wonder that cooking devices claiming to do just that (such as air fryers and electric pressure cookers) have risen in popularity in recent years.

In essence, an air fryer is a small convection oven. Its guarantee: it will have the same feel and taste as your beloved deep-fried dishes but without the calories and fat.

The countertop cooking equipment appears tempting, promising crispy, exactly like-fried perfection. Some are as tiny as toaster ovens and take up nearly the same amount of counter space. But what is an air fryer, how does it operate, do you need to use oil, and can it live up to the buzz? Keep reading to find out more!

Chapter 1. What Is an Air Fryer?

The air fryer is simply a countertop convection oven with more power. (However, there is a distinction to be made between baking and air-frying.) The compact gadget, patented by the Philips Electronics Company, promises to duplicate the effects of deep-frying using just hot air and almost no oil.

And according to market research company NPD Group, approximately 40% of houses in the United States have one as of July 2020. Everything from handmade French fries to prepackaged chicken wings and roasted veggies and fresh-baked cookies may be air-fried.

1.1. How Do Air Fryers Function?

Air fryers circulate hot air around the food item to achieve the same crispiness as conventional fried dishes. Air fryers can achieve this by eliminating high-calorie and high-fat oils from the cooking process. A person may get identical results to a deep fryer with a minute quantity of the fat and calories by using only 1 tbsp of cooking oil instead of numerous cups.

According to researchers, air fryers remove moisture from meals using heated air containing tiny oil droplets. Consequently, the product has qualities similar to fried dishes but with significantly decreased fat levels.

Like many other cooking processes, air-frying causes a chemical reaction called the Maillard effect, which enhances the color and taste of the meal.

1.2. Advantages of air fryers

When used correctly, air fryers provide lots of new health benefits:

Air fryers may help you lose weight.

Fried food consumption is directly linked to an increased risk of obesity. This is due to the high fat and calorie content of deep-fried dishes.

Weight reduction may be aided by converting from deep-fried to air-fried dishes and eliminating frequent consumption of unhealthy oils.

Deep fryers are not always as safe as air fryers.

Deep-frying meals necessitates the use of a big container filled with hot oil. This might be dangerous. While air fryers do become hot, there is no danger of splashing, spilling, or touching the boiling oil by mistake. To maintain safety, people should operate frying machines properly and follow instructions.

The danger of hazardous acrylamide production is reduced when using an air fryer.

Frying food in oil may result in hazardous chemicals like acrylamide. This chemical develops in some meals during high-heat cooking techniques, such as deep-frying.

Acrylamide has been linked to the formation of malignancies such as endometrial, pancreatic, ovarian, and esophageal and breast, cancer, according to the European Agency for Research on Cancer.

People may reduce the danger of acrylamide contamination in their meals by switching to air frying.

Reducing your intake of deep-fried meals lowers your risk of illness.

Ways to cook with oil and to eat traditional fried dishes on a daily basis have been linked to a variety of health problems. Deep frying may be replaced with alternative cooking techniques to lessen the risk of these consequences.

Chapter 2. How To Use an Air Fryer?

A heating mechanism and a fan are housed in the upper part of an air fryer. When you turn on the fryer, heated air flows down and around the food in a fryer-style basket. The food becomes crisp due to the quick circulation, which is similar to deep-frying but without the oil.

The following are some tips for using an air fryer:

1. Load the basket with your food.

The basket may accommodate anywhere from 2 to 10 quarts, depending on the size of your air fryer. In most circumstances, 1 or 2 tbsp of oil will be needed to help the meal get crispy.

2. Decide on a time and a temperature.

Depending on the item you are preparing, air fryer cooking durations and temperatures vary from 5 to 25 minutes at 350° to 400°F.

3. Allow the meal to cook.

To help the food crisping up uniformly, you may have to turn it or flip halfway during the cooking cycle. It is essential to clean the air fryer once you have finished cooking.

2.1. Which Air Fryer Is the Best?

Our Test Kitchen put various devices to the test to identify the finest air fryer, and three manufacturers came out on top. The Philips Advance Turbo-Star Air Fryer has long been our favorite, but the Power Vortex Air Fryer and the Black & Decker Purify Air Fryer also wowed our experts.

The cost of these devices varies based on their size and functionality. You may wish to purchase various air fryer accessories in addition to the equipment itself.

2.2. How to Wash an Air Fryer Completely

Collect your materials

Gather all of the required equipment and materials before you begin cleaning your air fryer. These are some of them:

- A soft bristle brush sponge
- A cleaning brush with gentle bristles
- Baking soda
- Tissue paper
- Dish soap

Allow Time for Your Air Fryer to Cool

Allow your air fryer to cool for at least 30 minutes after unplugging it. Remove any detachable pieces from the appliance after it has cooled (basket, tray, pan).

Remove the Removable Parts and Clean Them

Remove the detachable pieces and wash them in warm soapy water. "If you see baked-on oil or burned food on the components, soak them in warm soapy water for approximately 10 to 15 minutes, then clean them with a soft bristle brush sponge," Bedwyr advises. (Alternatively, you may put them in the dishwasher if they are dishwasher safe.)

Make a cleaning mixture of baking soda and water for any hard-to-clean portions of the fryer or stubborn food residue that will not come off. "With a soft-bristle brush, rub the paste onto the residue and wipe clean," Carson advises.

"With a soft-bristle brush, rub the paste onto the residue and wipe clean," Carson advises.

Cleaning the Interior

Clean the inside of the air fryer using a moist microfiber cloth or a soft bristle brush sponge dipped in dish soap. Then, using a clean wet towel, wipe away any soap residue.

Check the Heating Element

Wipe off the heating element of your air fryer with a moist cloth or a non-abrasive sponge.

Wipe the Outside

Wipe off the outside using a damp cloth and a little dish soap, just like the inside. Wipe away any soap residue with a clean moist cloth, then polish the exterior with a paper towel.

Put Your Air Fryer Back Together

Make sure your air fryer is completely dry in every nook and cranny. Put all the detachable pieces into the main unit, and there you have it! Your air fryer is all set to go.

Chapter 3. General Tips for Air Frying

It is essential for keeping your air fryer in good working order. Use the things listed below as a guide to continue creating delicious dishes.

3.1. Getting Ready to Air-Fry

Choose the best location in your kitchen for your air fryer. Always place your air fryer on a flat, heat-resistant tabletop with at least 5 inches of clearance behind it where the air vent is placed.

Before putting your meal in the air fryer, be sure it is hot. It is simple: preheat the air fryer to the desired temperature and set a timer for two or three minutes. The air fryer is preheated and ready for food when the timer goes off.

Make sure you have the correct accessories. You may want to purchase some additions for your new favorite gadget once you start air frying. You could already have some. As long as they do not come into proximity with the heating source, any oven-safe cake pans, or baking dishes should work in an air fryer. The only need is that the accessory pan fits within the air fryer basket.

Purchase a spray bottle for the kitchen. Spraying oil on food is simpler than drizzling or brushing, and it uses less oil in the long run. While oil sprays in cans are available, they can include aerosol agents that may damage the non-stick surface of your air fryer basket. Get a hand-pumped kitchen spray bottle if you wish to spray meals straight into the basket. It will be well worth it!

Make a sling out of aluminum foil. Getting accessory components into and out of the air fryer basket might be difficult. Fold a piece of aluminum foil into a strip approximately 2-inches wide by 24-inches long to make it simpler. Set the cake pan or baking dish on the foil, then raise the pan or dish and drop it into the air fryer basket by holding the foil ends. Return the air fryer basket to the air fryer after folding or tucking the aluminum foil ends into the basket. When ready to take the pan from the air fryer basket, unfold the aluminum foil and hold onto the ends to pull it out.

Make sure you are using the right breading process. In many air fryer recipes, breading is a key step. Make sure you do not miss any steps! It is critical to cover meals first in flour, then in egg, and last in breadcrumbs. Keep a close eye on the breadcrumbs and use your hands to push them onto the meal. So, because the air fryer's mechanism includes a strong fan, breading may sometimes fly off the meal. The breading will adhere better if the crumbs are pressed in firmly.

3.2. While Air Frying the Food

When frying fatty items, add water to the air fryer drawer. Putting water in the drawer under the basket prevents the grease from becoming too hot and smoking. When frying bacon, sausage, or very fatty burgers, do this.

Make sure the basket is not too full. This is something I cannot emphasize enough. While it is tempting to cook more at once, overloading the basket will hinder dishes from crispy texture and browning evenly, taking longer overall.

Halfway through the cooking period, turn the ingredients over. You must flip things over to brown evenly, just like you would if you were cooking on a grill or in a pan.

To check for doneness, open the air fryer as frequently as you wish. One of the nicest features of air fryers is that you may open the drawer as frequently as you like (within limits) to check on the progress of the frying process. It will not harm the air fryer; the fryer will both continue timing and heating while you remove the basket or resume where it stopped when you replace the basket with the fryer.

To keep meals in place, use toothpicks. The blower from the air fryer will sometimes take up light meals and blow them about. So, use toothpicks to fasten meals (such as the top piece of bread on a sandwich).

Shake the basket a little bit. During the cooking time, shake the basket several times to redistribute the contents and help them brown and crisp more evenly.

Partway through, spray with oil. Try spritzing the meal with oil halfway through the cooking process if you want to be brown and crisp up more. This will also aid in the uniform browning of the food.

3.3. After Air-Frying

Before putting out items, take the air fryer basket from the drawer. This is crucial, and you will only make this mistake once. If you flip the basket while it is still secured into the air fryer drawer, all of the released fat or surplus oil will wind up on your plate, along with the item you just air fried.

Do not spill the fluids out of the drawer too quickly. The drawer underneath the air fryer basket absorbs a lot of liquids from the cooked dishes above it, as well as any sauces you pour over it. You may use these tasty juices as a sauce to pour over the dish if the drippings are not too oily. To concentrate the taste, degrease the liquid and reduce it in a small pot on heat for a few minutes.

After each usage, clean both the drawer and the basket. Do not put off cleaning the air fryer's drawer since it is simple. You face the danger of food contamination if you do not wash it, and your kitchen will stink in a day or two!

Allow the air fryer to dry on its own. Simply place the air fryer drawer and basket back into it and put it on for a few minutes after cleaning them. This is much superior to using a drying towel to dry both portions.**3.4. Food Reheating in An Air-Fryer**

Because leftovers vary so much, there is no hard and fast rule for reheating them in terms of time and temperature. I recommend reheating the food in the air fryer at 350°F for as long as it takes to reach a safe temperature of 160°F. This is particularly critical for meals that might be dangerous, such as beef, poultry, and pig.

Chapter 4. Frequently Asked Questions about Air Fryer

Here are some FAQs usually asked by users:

1. Is air-fried food good for you?

Air-fried food might be argued to be healthier than deep-fried food since it requires less oil. In contrast to deep-fried French fries, which have a staggering 17 grams of fat per serving, frozen French fries heated in an air fryer have between 4 and 7 grams of fat per serving.

2. What are the advantages and disadvantages of air fryers?

Advantages: Air fryers make it simple to heat up frozen dishes and that too in a somewhat healthier way than deep-frying. The results are much superior to those obtained by conventional frying, and your kitchen stays cool.

Disadvantages: Even the biggest air fryers have a limited capacity, so you will have to cook in batches—especially if you are feeding a crowd. Air fryers are larger than a toaster and take up precious counter space. Finally, depending on the model, they might be costly.

3. Is it worthwhile to invest in an air fryer?

With so many variants on the market, the price of this popular appliance has dropped in recent years—many models are around $200, and others are under $100. Still, buying an air fryer is probably only worthwhile if you often prepare fried dishes (frozen or handmade)

AIR FRYER RECIPES

CHICKEN BREAST

INGREDIENTS

- 1 POUND OR 2 CHICKEN BREASTS, BONELESS AND SKINLESS
- ¼ TSP GROUND BLACK PEPPER
- ½ TSP PAPRIKA
- ½ TSP SALT
- ½ TSP GARLIC POWDER
- ½ TSP ITALIAN SEASONING
- ½ TBSP VEGETABLE OIL

25 MINUTES — 2 SERVINGS

Instructions:

- Press the chicken breasts totally dry with a paper towel.
- Smear a generous amount of oil all over the chicken.
- Season the chicken equally with all seasonings, including pepper, salt, Italian seasoning, garlic powder and paprika.
- Add the seasonings and chicken in a big Ziploc bag, then shake thoroughly to coat. Put aside to marinate for at least 15 min or refrigerate up overnight.
- In the air fryer basket, arrange the marinated chicken breasts in a single layer.
- Cook for 22 to 25 minutes at 375°F until the chicken is thoroughly cooked and the internal temperature reaches 160°F. Stick a meat thermometer into the thickest breast section to check the internal temperature.
- Allow for 5-10 min of resting time in the air fryer before plating.

Nutritional Value: *Calories 350kcal | Protein 61.4g | Fat 9.5g | Carbs0.9g | Salt 510.7mg |Sugar 0.1g |Fibers 0g*

SWEET CHILI CHICKEN BITES

INGREDIENTS

- ½ LB. CHICKEN BREASTS, SKINLESS AND BONELESS
- ½ TSP CRUSHED BLACK PEPPER
- 1/8 CUP OF ALL-PURPOSE FLOUR
- ½ TBSP SALT
- 1 CUP BREADCRUMBS
- ½ TSP PAPRIKA
- 1 EGG, BEATEN
- ¼ CUP OF SWEET CHILI SAUCE, STORE-BOUGHT OR HOMEMADE
- COOKING OIL SPRAY

30 MINUTES 2 SERVINGS

For garnish:

- ½ tsp sesame seeds (white)
- ½ tbsp green onions, chopped finely

For sweet chili sauce(homemade):

- 1/8 cup of rice vinegar
- ½ tbsp soy sauce (or fish sauce)
- 1 tbsp brown sugar
- ½ tsp flour (or cornstarch)
- 1 tbsp chili garlic sauce (or sambal oelek)
- 1 tbsp water

Instructions:

- Cut the chicken breasts into 1-inch cubes after properly drying them with a paper towel. Season to taste with paprika, salt, and pepper, in a medium mixing bowl. Put aside for about 5 min.

- Combine flour and chicken pieces in a big Ziploc bag. To coat, seal the package and shake it vigorously.
- Take a shallow plate containing beaten eggs and a deeper plate with breadcrumbs. One at a time, dip the chicken into the beaten egg and coat it evenly. Then coat completely with breadcrumbs. To bind and properly coat each piece, gently press crumbs into it.
- Inside this air fryer basket, arrange the chicken bites in a single layer and lightly spray with oil to coat evenly. Cook for 12 to 14 minutes at 375 degrees Fahrenheit, or till golden brown and the temperature of the chicken reaches 168 F. To uniformly brown the chicken bits, shake the basket halfway through cooking.
- Add the sweet chili sauce to the cooked chicken in a big mixing bowl (or if preparing homemade sweet chili sauce, add the chicken into the saucepan after the sauce has been cooked and thickened). Toss lightly and well to completely coat. Green onions and sesame seeds are sprinkled on top.
- To prepare your own sweet chili sauce:
- In a medium-sized mixing bowl, combine vinegar, brown sugar, fish sauce, sambal oelek, water and cornstarch. Whisk together until the sugar and cornstarch are completely dissolved.
- Pour the sauce into a small saucepan and cook for 3 to 4 minutes over medium heat. Stir until the mixture has thickened to the desired consistency.

Nutritional Value: Calories 483 | Protein 37.8g | Fat 12.4g | Carbs 52.7g | Salt 2683.5mg | Sugar 8.1g | Fibers 3g

BUFFALO CHICKEN WINGS

INGREDIENTS

- 12 WINGS
- 1 TSP ONION POWDER
- ½ TBSP GROUND BLACK PEPPER
- ½ CUP OLIVE OIL
- 1 TSP GARLIC POWDER
- FOR BUFFALO WING SAUCE
- 1/4 CUP MARGARINE
- 1/2 CUP LOUISIANA HOT SAUCE
- 1 TSP PAPRIKA
- 2 TBSP WATER
- 1/8 TSP GARLIC POWDER
- 2 TSP GRANULATED SUGAR
- 1/8 TSP ONION POWDER

22 MINUTES   2 SERVINGS

Sauce for chicken wings:

- In a saucepan, combine all of the ingredients for the sauce and cook over medium heat then take off the heat and set aside for 5 minutes to cool.
- Combine the completely cooked wings and the sauce in a medium mixing dish.

Instructions:

- Heat the Air Fryer to about 180 degrees Celsius (360 degrees Fahrenheit). Get the basket ready.
- In a big sealable plastic bag, combine the wings, spices, and olive oil. Toss the wings in the bag to coat them with oil and spices uniformly. Add a sprinkle of baking powder to the wings before cooking to make them extra crispy.
- Arrange the wings in a proper layer in the air fryer basket that has been prepared. Cook for 18 mins at 360 degrees, turning the wings every 5 to 6 mins. Cook for 2 mins after increasing the temperature to 390 degrees Fahrenheit.

Nutritional Value: *Calories 1358kcal | Protein 54g | Fat 123g | Carbs 9g | Salt 2068mg |Sugar 5g |Fibers 1g*

HEALTHY CHICKEN AND VEGGIES

INGREDIENTS

- 1/2-POUND CHICKEN BREAST, CHOPPED INTO BITE-SIZE PIECES (2 MEDIUM-SIZED CHICKEN BREASTS)
- 1 /2 CUP OF BROCCOLI FLORETS (FRESH OR FROZEN)
- ½ ZUCCHINI CHOPPED
- ½ CUP OF BELL PEPPER CHOPPED (ANY COLORS YOU LIKE)
- 1/4 ONION CHOPPED
- 1 CLOVES GARLIC MINCED OR CRUSHED
- 1 TBSP OLIVE OIL
- 1/4 TSP EACH OF CHILI POWDER, GARLIC POWDER, PEPPER, SALT,
- ½ TBSP ITALIAN SEASONING (OR SPICE BLEND OF CHOICE)

15 MINUTES   2 SERVINGS

Instructions:

- Preheat the air fryer to 400 degrees Fahrenheit. Put the chopped vegetables and chicken into tiny bite-size pieces in a large mixing dish.
- Toss the oil and spices together into the mixing dish with chicken and veggies.
- Cook the seasoned vegetables and chicken for 10 minutes in the air fryers, shaking halfway through, or until the chicken and vegetables are browned and the poultry is cooked through in the preheated air fryer. If your air fryer is not big enough, you might have to cook them in two or three batches.
- Veggies: Use your favorite quick-cooking vegetables in lieu of the vegetables. The air fryer may be used to cook potatoes.
- First, boil the potatoes for 10 minutes.
- Spices: use your preferred spice combination for the Italian seasoning. Taco, lemon pepper, Cajun, or any other flavor combination works well. If the mix already contains salt, make sure to cut back on the salt.

Nutritional Value: Calories 230kcal | Protein 26g | Fat 10g | Carbs 8g Salt 437mg |Sugar 4g |Fibers 3g

SPICY CHICKEN AND BROCCOLI

INGREDIENTS

- 1/2 LB. SKINLESS, BONELESS CHICKEN THIGHS OR BREAST, CUT INTO BITES SIZED PIECES (AROUND 1-INCH)
- 1 SMALL ONION, THICK SLICES
- 1 CUP BROCCOLI FLORETS
- 1/4 TSP GARLIC POWDER
- 1 TBSP FRESH MINCED GINGER
- 1 ½ TBSP GRAPESEED OIL OR OLIVE OIL
- 1 TBSP TAMARI FOR GLUTEN FREE, OR TO TASTE (USE LOW SODIUM SOY SAUCE)
- 1 TSP SESAME OIL
- 1 TBSP RICE VINEGAR
- 1 TSP HOT SAUCE (OPTIONAL)
- LEMON WEDGES, FOR SERVING (OPTIONAL)
- BLACK PEPPER, TO TASTE
- 1/4 TSP SEA SALT, OR TO TASTE

15 MINUTES   2 SERVINGS

Instructions

- Combine the oil, ginger, garlic powder, soy sauce, sesame oil, rice vinegar, optional spicy sauce, pepper, and salt, in a large mixing bowl to make the marinade.
- Marinate the chicken and broccoli. Put the chicken in a separate bowl. In a separate bowl, combine the broccoli and onions. Distribute the marinade in between two bowls and toss to evenly coat each.
- Place only the chicken in the tray or basket of an air fryer. Air fry for 10 minutes at 195°C/380°F. Then combine the broccoli and onions with the chicken into the mixing bowl (make sure to include all the marinade). Return all the ingredients into the Air Fryer for another 8-10 minutes at 380°F/195°C, or until the chicken is cooked through. Stir halfway during cooking to ensure that the broccoli is uniformly cooked.
- Season with salt and pepper to taste. Serve warm with a squeeze of fresh lemon juice on top if desired.

Nutritional Value: Calories 224kcal | Protein 25g | Fat 11g | Carbs 4g | Salt 619mg | Sugar 1g | Fibers 1g

HEALTHY PORK CHOPS

INGREDIENTS

- 2 PORK CHOPS CUT THICK
- ¼ TSP PAPRIKA
- ¼ TSP ONION POWDER
- ¼ TSP BLACK PEPPER
- 1/8 TSP GARLIC POWDER

15 MINUTES — 2 SERVINGS

Instructions

- Heat the Air Fryer at 400 degrees F.
- Combine the ingredients in a small bowl, then spread the seasoning all over the pork chops with your hands, completely coating each chop's front, back, and sides.
- Prep the Air Fryer basket with a non-stick spray or baking paper, and then arrange the pork chops in a single layer in the base of the air fryer basket. Ensure there is enough space between each pork chop for air to circulate.
- Cook for 6 minutes at 400°F. Cook for a further 8 to 10 minutes after flipping the pork chops. Before removing the meat, insert a meat thermometer to ensure that the temperature inside the meat has reached 145 degrees Fahrenheit. If more time is required, add it in 2-minute intervals.
- Serve right away with your favorite sides.

Nutritional Value: *Calories 210kcal | Protein 29g | Fat 9g | Carbs 1g*

Salt 65mg |Sugar 1g |Fibers 1g

ITALIAN PORK CHOPS

INGREDIENTS

- 2 PIECES OF BONELESS PORK CHOPS, 1/2-INCH THICK
- ½ TBSP OLIVE OIL
- ½ TSP PAPRIKA
- ¼ TSP SALT
- ½ TSP ONION POWDER
- ½ TSP GARLIC POWDER
- 1/4 TSP ITALIAN SEASONING
- 1/8 TSP GROUND BLACK PEPPER

15 MINUTES   2 SERVINGS

Instructions

- Mix the spice ingredients in a bowl: Italian seasoning, salt, garlic powder, paprika, onion powder, and pepper,
- Heat the air fryer for 5 mins at 380°F.
- Season the pork chops with the spice mix after coating them with oil on both sides.
- Air fries the pork chops at 380°F for around 10-15 minutes, or until they reach 145°F. Halfway through the cooking time, flip the pork chops.
- Let it rest for a few minutes before serving.

Nutritional Value: Calories 284kcal | Protein 33g | Fat 15g | Carbs 2g | Salt 462mg | Sugar 1g | Fibers 1g

ASIAN PORK MEATBALLS

INGREDIENTS

- 1/3 LB. GROUND CHICKEN (IF POSSIBLE DARK MEAT)
- 1/3 LB. GROUND PORK
- 1 CLOVES GARLIC GRATED
- 1 STALK GREEN ONIONS FINELY CHOPPED
- 1 EGG WHISKED
- 1 SHITAKE MUSHROOMS FINELY CHOPPED
- 1 TBSP CILANTRO FINELY CHOPPED
- 1/4-INCH GINGER GRATED
- 1/4 TBSP SEA SALT
- 1 TBSP COCONUT AMINOS OR LIGHT SOY SAUCE
- OIL SPRAY

15 MINUTES 2 SERVINGS

For Garnish

- radishes sliced finely
- 1 head of butter leaf lettuce
- green onion chopped finely
- avocado sliced
- lime in wedges
- sesame seeds

For Dipping Sauce

- 1 tbsp fish sauce
- ½ cup coconut aminos or light soy sauce
- ¼ tbsp ginger grated
- ½ tbsp rice wine vinegar
- ¼ lime juiced

- ½ clove garlic grated

Instructions:

Prepare Dipping Sauce

- In a small bowl, mix together all of the ingredients. Allow marinating as you prepare the meatballs.

Prepare Asian Pork Meatballs

- In a large mixing bowl, combine all ingredients and mix well with your hands.
- Form roughly 10-14 meatballs (depending on how large or tiny you want them) into 1.5-inch balls using an ice cream or cookie scoop and place them on a platter.
- Cooking spray should be used to lightly oil the air fryer basket. Place the meatballs in the air fryer basket, being careful not to overcrowd them (work in batches).
- Cook for 8 to 12 minutes at 400 F in an air fryer. Cook for about 8 minutes if your meatballs are less than 1 inch, and 10 to 12 minutes if they are larger. Take one from the air fryer to assess for tenderness, crispiness, and other preferences. Try giving them an additional minute or two if needed.
- Enjoy on top of Asian noodles with stir-fry veggies with a sauce and fresh avocado, radishes, sesame seeds and green onions in lettuce cups.

Nutritional Values: Calories 386kcal | Protein 27g | Fat 29g | Carbs 4g | Salt 391mg |Sugar 1g |Fibers 0g

YUMMY PORK ROAST

INGREDIENTS

- 1/3 PORK LOIN JOINT
- 1/2 TSP SALT

40 MINUTES 2 SERVINGS

Instructions

- Cut the rind along its length. The rind can be difficult to cut through, so use a sharp knife with caution. Make certain not to cut down on the fat and flesh underneath the rind.
- Dry the rind with a clean towel and liberally salt it. Make a point of rubbing salt into the incisions you just made. Then, allow the pork roast to rest, skin side up, in the refrigerator for about 24 hours. Take a glance at it once or twice while it is resting and wipe away any liquid that develops. This will guarantee that the rind completely dries off.
- Heat your air fryer at 400 degrees Fahrenheit / 200 degrees Celsius.
- Place the pork roast, skin side up, in the air fryer and cook until the inner temperature of the meat reaches 145 F / 63 C. The precise roasting time will differ according to the weight of the meat.
- Take the roasted pork roast out of the air fryer and set it aside for 15 minutes before carving and serving.

Nutritional Values: Calories 483 kcal | Protein 82g | Fat 15g | Carbs 6g | Salt 954mg | Sugar 2g | Fibers 1g

EASY PULLED PORK

INGREDIENTS

- 1/2 LB. PORK SHOULDER, BONELESS
- 1 TBSP OF PORK LION SEASONING
- 1 TBSP OLIVE OIL
- SALT
- FRESH PEPPER

90 MINUTES 2 SERVINGS

Instructions

- Using olive oil, brush the pork shoulder
- Use a small bowl to blend all spices or use ready-made pork seasoning.
- Sprinkle the meat with the pork seasoning. Rub the pork with your hands to get the spice into the flesh.
- Heat the Air Fryer for 3 minutes at 375°F. Place the pork in an Air Fryer cake barrel or cake pans so that the fluids from the meat remain in the barrel.
- Setup the timer for 40 minutes and flip the pork after 15 minutes as it cooks.
- Inspect the thickest portion of the pork to determine whether it is 180°F; if not, add 15 minutes to the cooking time.
- Once the cooking time is up, keep the pork in the Air Fryer for about 30 minutes to allow the meat to rest. The pork continues to roast and rest while the Air Fryer cools.
- Then, remove the pork from the Air Fryer and rip it apart with two forks.

Nutritional Values: Calories 409kcal | Protein 28g | Fat 32g | Carbs 0g | Salt 322mg |Sugar 0g |Fibers 0g

JUICY TURKEY BURGERS

INGREDIENTS

- 1/2 LB. GROUND TURKEY 85/15
- ¼ ONION GRATED
- 2 TBSP CUP UNSWEETENED APPLE SAUCE
- 1 TSP WORCESTERSHIRE SAUCE
- 3 TSP RANCH SEASONING
- 1/8 CUP PLAIN BREADCRUMBS
- 1/2 TSP MINCED GARLIC
- PEPPER AND SALT TO TASTE

15 MINUTES 2 SERVINGS

Instructions:

- Combine the ground turkey, onion, unsweetened apple sauce, Worchester sauce, ranch seasoning, minced garlic, breadcrumbs, pepper, and salt in a mixing bowl.
- Blend with your hands until everything is incorporated. Make 4 equal-sized hamburger patties.
- After that, put your burgers in the fridge for approximately 30 minutes to firm up a little.
- Heat your Air Fryer at 360 °F by running it on that setting for approximately 3 minutes. Put your burgers in the Air fryer, being careful not to overlap or overlap. Cook for 15 mins at 360°F, turning halfway through. When your burgers reach an inner temperature of 168 f on a quick read thermometer, they are done.
- *For frozen burgers, insert burger in prepared air fryer basket and cook for 18 mins on 360 F, turning halfway through.
- *A little oil on the air fryer basket might help keep it from sticking.

Nutritional Values: Calories 179kcal | Protein 28g | Fat 3g | Carbs 11g | Salt 419mg | Sugar 3g | Fibers 1g

HEALTHY TURKEY BREAST

INGREDIENTS

- 1 POUND ON THE BONE TURKEY BREAST WITH SKIN (RIBS REMOVED)
- 1/8 TBSP. DRY POULTRY OR TURKEY SEASONING
- 1/2 TSP KOSHER SALT
- 2 TSP OLIVE OIL

55 MINUTES   2 SERVINGS

Instructions:

- Rub a half-tsp of oil over the turkey breast. Sprinkle both surfaces with salt and turkey spice before rubbing in the other half tbsp of olive oil on the skin side.
- Heat the air fryer to 350°F and cook the skin side down for 20 minutes, then flip and cook till the inner temperature of the breast reaches 160°F with an instant-read thermometer, roughly 30 to 40 minutes longer determined by the size of the breast. Allow it to rest for 10 minutes before cutting.

Nutritional Values: Calories 226kcal | Protein 32.5 | Fat 10 | Carbs 6g | Salt 296mg | Sugar 6g | Fibers 2g

TASTY TURKEY MEATBALLS

INGREDIENTS

- 3/4 LB. (675G) TURKEY MINCE
- 1 SMALL EGG BEAT LIGHTLY
- ½ RED BELL PEPPER DESEED AND CHOP FINELY
- 2 TSP FRESH CORIANDER OR CILANTRO MINCED
- 2 TBSP PARSLEY OR FRESH HERBS MINCED
- BLACK PEPPER
- SALT
- COOKING SPRAY

10 MINUTES **2 SERVINGS**

Instructions:

- Heat the air fryer to 400°F/200°C.
- In a mixing dish, combine all ingredients (excluding the cooking spray).
- Form into 1-1/4-inch meatballs.
- Place half of the meatballs in an air fryer basket in a single layer; cook for 7 to 10 minutes, or until golden brown and cooked thoroughly (shaking halfway through).
- Repeat with the remaining meatballs, removing and keeping warm.
- Serve with toothpicks and sauce while still warm.

Nutritional Values: *Calories 220kcal | Protein 42g | Fat 4g | Carbs 2g | Salt 111mg | Sugar 1g | Fibers 1g*

TURKEY TENDERLOIN BAKED

INGREDIENTS

- ½ LB. OF TURKEY TENDERLOINS
- 3 TSP ITALIAN SEASONING
- PEPPER AND SALT TO TASTE
- FRESH PARSLEY FOR GARNISHING

25 MINUTES   2 SERVINGS

Instructions:

- Heat the air fryer to 350°F.
- Season the turkey with Italian seasoning, salt, and pepper.
- Cook the turkey tenderloins in the air fryer for 25 minutes, turning once. The tenderloin should be cooked to an internal temperature of 165°F.
- Take the turkey out of the air fryer and set aside for 5 minutes to rest until slicing.

Nutritional Values: Calories 168kcal | Protein 34g | Fat 2g | Carbs 0g | Salt 162mg | Sugar 0g | Fibers 0g

HEALTHY TURKEY CROQUETTES

INGREDIENTS

- 1 CUP OF MASHED POTATOES (WITH MILK AND BUTTER ADDED)
- 1/4 CUP OF SHREDDED SWISS CHEESE
- 1/4 CUP OF GRATED PARMESAN CHEESE
- 1/2 SHALLOT, CHOP FINELY
- 1 TSP FRESH SAGE MINCED, OR 1/4 TSP SAGE LEAVES DRIED
- 1 TSP FRESH ROSEMARY MINCED, OR 1/2 TSP CRUSHED DRIED ROSEMARY,
- 1/8 TSP PEPPER
- 1/4 TSP SALT
- 1 CUP OF COOKED TURKEY CHOPPED FINELY
- 1 SMALL EGG
- 1-CUP PANKO BREADCRUMBS
- SOUR CREAM, OPTIONAL
- COOKING SPRAY (BUTTER-FLAVORED)

10 MINUTES   2 SERVINGS

Instructions:

- Heat the air fryer to 350 degrees Fahrenheit. Mix mashed potatoes, shallot, cheeses, rosemary, salt, pepper, and sage, in a large mixing bowl; mix in turkey. Lightly but completely combine all ingredients. Form into 4 1-inch-thick patties.
- Whisk together the egg and water in a small dish. In a separate shallow dish, combine the breadcrumbs. Dip the croquettes into the egg mixture and then in the breadcrumbs, pressing them down to help the coating stick.
- Work in batches, arrange croquettes in an air-fryer basket in a single layer on an oiled tray, spray with cooking spray. Cook for 4-5 minutes, or until golden brown. Cooking spray should be sprayed on the turn. Cook for 4-5 minutes, or until golden brown. Serve alongside sour cream if preferred.

Nutritional Values: Calories 322kcal | Protein 29g | Fat 12g | Carbs 22g | Salt 673mg | Sugar 2g | Fibers 2g

ROAST-STYLE BABY POTATOES

INGREDIENTS

- ½ LB. BABY POTATOES, CUT IN HALF
- 3 TSP OLIVE OIL
- 1/2 TSP GARLIC POWDER
- ¼ TBSP PAPRIKA
- 1/2 TSP OLD BAY SEASONING (OR ITALIAN SEASONING)
- 1/2 TSP SOY SAUCE
- 1/2 TSP BALSAMIC VINEGAR
- 1/2 TSP CRUSHED BLACK PEPPER
- 1/2 TSP SALT

20 MINUTES   2 SERVINGS

Instructions:

- Heat the air fryer to 350 degrees Fahrenheit. Mix mashed potatoes, shallot, cheeses, rosemary, salt, pepper, and sage, in a large mixing bowl; mix in turkey. Lightly but completely combine all ingredients. Form into 4 1-inch-thick patties.
- Whisk together the egg and water in a small dish. In a separate shallow dish, combine the breadcrumbs. Dip the croquettes into the egg mixture and then in the breadcrumbs, pressing them down to help the coating stick.
- Work in batches, arrange croquettes in an air-fryer basket in a single layer on an oiled tray, spray with cooking spray. Cook for 4-5 minutes, or until golden brown. Cooking spray should be sprayed on the turn. Cook for 4-5 minutes, or until golden brown. Serve alongside sour cream if preferred.

Nutritional Values: Calories 118kcal | Protein 2.4g | Fat 3.8g | Carbs 19.9g | Salt 637.5mg |Sugar 1.7g |Fibers 2g

HEALTHY HASH BROWNS

INGREDIENTS
- 2 FROZEN HASH BROWN PATTIES

10 MINUTES | 2 SERVINGS

Instructions:

- Arrange the frozen patties inside the air fryer basket or on the air fryer tray to start. Do not allow them to stack or overlap.
- Cook for 10 to12 minutes at 400 ° F.
- Halfway through cooking, turn the patties. Cooking time should be increased by 2 to 4 minutes for crispier patties

Nutritional Values: Calories 1 kcal | Protein 1g | Fat 1g | Carbs 1g | Salt 1mg|Sugar 1g|Fibers 1g

CHEESY BUFFALO CAULIFLOWERS BITES

INGREDIENTS

- 2 CUPS OF CAULIFLOWER FLORETS
- 3 TSP OLIVE OIL EXTRA VIRGIN
- 1/4 TSP SALT
- 1/8 TSP PEPPER
- 3 TBSP BUFFALO SAUCE
- 1/4 CUP OF SHREDDED SHARP CHEDDAR CHEESE

10 MINUTES 2 SERVINGS

Instructions:

- Season the cauliflower with salt and pepper after tossing it with olive oil.
- Arrange the cauliflower in a uniform layer in the tray of an air fryer.
- Cook, tossing the basket once through, for 9 minutes.
- Take out the cauliflower and combine it with the Buffalo sauce in a mixing bowl.
- Put the cauliflower back into the air fryer basket and sprinkle it with the cheddar cheese.
- Place the basket in the air fryer for an additional 1-2 mins, just until the cheese melts.
- Serve the cauliflower on a platter with Ranch dressing, if preferred.

Nutritional Values: Calories 171kcal | Protein 9g | Fat 13g | Carbs 5g | Salt 1110mg | Sugar 2g | Fibers 2g

CRISPY VEGETABLES

INGREDIENTS

- 1/2 RED BELL PEPPER CHOPPED
- 1/4 CUP OF ZUCCHINI SLICED INTO ½" MOONS
- 1/2 CUP OF MUSHROOMS HALVED
- ½ TBSP OLIVE OIL
- CLOVES GARLIC MINCED
- PEPPER & SALT TO TASTE
- ½ TBSP PARMESAN CHEESE GRATED
- ¼ TSP ITALIAN SEASONING

10 MINUTES   2 SERVINGS

Instructions:

- Heat the air fryer to 375 °F.
- Toss together all ingredients except the parmesan cheese.
- Set in the air fryer in a uniform layer
- Cook for 6 minutes, mix and top with parmesan.
- Cook for another 3ot5 minutes, or until the potatoes are soft and crisp.

Nutritional Values: Calories 58kcal | Protein 2g | Fat 4g | Carbs 4g | Salt 25mg | Sugar 2g | Fibers 1g

STUFFED SWEET POTATOES

INGREDIENTS

- 1 MEDIUM SWEET POTATO
- 1/2 TSP OLIVE OIL
- 1/2 CUP OF CHEDDAR CHEESE, SHREDDED AND DIVIDED
- 1/2 CUP OF CHOPPED SPINACH, COOKED AND DRAINED
- 1 COOKED BACON STRIP, CRUMBLED
- 1/2 GREEN ONION, CUT INTO SMALL PIECES
- 1/8 CUP OF PECANS, TOASTED AND CHOPPED
- 1/8 CUP OF FRESH CRANBERRIES, CHOPPED COARSELY
- 1 TBSP BUTTER
- 1/8 TSP PEPPER
- 1/8 TSP KOSHER SALT

45 MINUTES 2 SERVINGS

Instructions:

- Heat the air fryer to 400 °F. Brush the potatoes with olive oil. Place in the air fryer basket on an ungreased tray. Cook for 30-to 40 minutes, or until potatoes are cooked; allow to cool.
- Potatoes should be cut in half lengthwise. Scrape out the pulp, keeping a 1/4-inch-thick casing. Mash the pulp in a big mixing dish; mix the spinach, 3/4 cup cheese, bacon, onion, nuts, cranberries, butter, salt, and pepper. Drop into potato shells, slightly mounding.
- Reduce the heat to 360 degrees. Place potato halves in the air fryer basket, cut side up. Cook for ten minutes. Cook until the last 1/4 cup cheese is melted, for about 1-2 minutes.

Nutritional Values: *Calories 376kcal | Protein 12g | Fat 25g | Carbs 28g | Salt 489mg |Sugar 10g |Fibers 5g*

AIR FRIED FILET MIGNON

INGREDIENTS

- 2 (4-6 OUNCES EACH) FILET MIGNON
- 1 TBSP OLIVE OIL
- ½ TSP SALT
- ½ TSP PEPPER
- GARLIC HERB BUTTER, BLUE CHEESE BUTTER, OR GARLIC BUTTER OPTIONAL

12 MINUTES 2 SERVINGS

Instructions:

- To make the fillets, pat them dry and then brush them with oil on both the upper and bottom parts of each piece.
- Then, depending on your taste, sprinkle with pepper and salt.
- Place the steaks in the air fryer container. Air fry for 10 - 12 mins at 380 degrees F. Halfway through cooking, flip the steaks.
- To ensure the desired degree of doneness, use a meat thermometer. Allow the steak to rest for 5-10 minutes after cooking for added tenderness.

The precise cook time will be determined by how good you like your steak and the wattage of the air fryer.

We wanted medium-rare steaks, so we air-fried them for 6 mins on both sides. Use a meat thermometer to check the meat temperature.

Nutritional Values: Calories 1058kcal | Protein 62g | Fat 88g | Carbs 1g | Salt 1330mg |Sugar 1g |Fibers 1g

EASY MONGOLIAN BEEF

INGREDIENTS

- ½ LB. FLANK STEAK
- 1/8 CUP OF CORN STARCH
- FOR THE SAUCE
- 1 TSP VEGETABLE OIL
- 1/4 TBSP GARLIC MINCED
- 1/8 TSP GINGER
- 1/4 CUP OF GLUTEN-FREE SOY SAUCE
- 1/4 CUP OF BROWN SUGAR PACKED
- 1/4 CUP OF WATER

20 MINUTES   2 SERVINGS

For the Meat:

- ½ lb. Flank Steak
- 1/8 Cup of Corn Starch

For the Sauce:

- 1 tsp Vegetable Oil
- 1/4 tbsp Garlic Minced
- 1/8 tsp Ginger
- 1/4 Cup of Gluten-Free Soy Sauce
- 1/4 Cup of Brown Sugar Packed
- 1/4 Cup of Water

Extras:

- Cooked Rice

- Green Onions
- Green Beans

Instructions:

- Slice the steak thinly lengthwise, then sprinkle with corn starch.
- Cook for 5 minutes on both sides in the Air Fryer at 390°F. (Begin with 5 minutes and increase the time as needed this was cooked for 10 minutes on both sides; however, you can cook for less if u don't want well done)
- As the steak is cooking, warm up all the sauce ingredients in a medium skillet over medium-high heat.
- Stir all of the ingredients well until they come to a gentle boil.
- When both the steak and the sauce are done, lay the steak in a bowl, pour other sauce over and soak for 5 to-10 minutes.
- Once ready to serve, lift the steak with tongs and allow the excess sauce to drip off.
- Lay the steak on top of the cooked green beans and rice and drizzle with more sauce if desired

Nutritional Values: Calories 554kcal | Protein 44g | Fat 16g | Carbs 57g | Salt 2211mg |Sugar 35g |Fibers 1g

GARLIC BUTTER STEAKS

INGREDIENTS

- 2 SIRLOIN RIBEYE'S OR STEAKS 6OZ EACH
- 1 CLOVE OF GARLIC
- 1/2 TSP ROSEMARY DRIED
- 2 TBSP BUTTER UNSALTED
- 1/2 TSP PARSLEY DRIED
- PEPPER & SALT
- ALUMINUM FOIL

25 MINUTES | 2 SERVINGS

Instructions:

- Season the steaks with pepper and salt and set aside for about 2 hours until cooking. (They should have been defrosted.)
- While they are sitting, put the butter in a dish.
- Squeeze the garlic into the butter, then stir in the rosemary and parsley.
- Allow this to settle for a few minutes to allow the butter to melt.
- When ready to cook, put each steak into the air fryer basket.
- Cook for 10 minutes at 400°F.
- Rotate the steaks carefully and cook for another 5 to 10 minutes on the other side, or until done to your liking.
- When cooked, lay out two pieces of foil and place a steak in each.
- Place half of the butter on each steak and close the foil around it to 'tent' the steaks.
- Allow this to settle for 5 minutes.

Nutritional Values: Calories 519kcal | Protein 46g | Fat 36g | Carbs 1g | Salt 245mg | Sugar 0g | Fibers 0g

STEAK BITES & MUSHROOMS

INGREDIENTS

- 1/2 LB. OF SIRLOIN STEAKS, CHOPPED INTO 1/2" CUBES
- 4 OZ. MUSHROOMS HALVED
- 1/2 TSP WORCESTERSHIRE SAUCE
- 1 TBSP MELTED BUTTER (OR OLIVE OIL)
- 1/4 TSP GARLIC POWDER, IF PREFERRED
- BLACK PEPPER FRESHLY CRACKED, TO TASTE
- FLAKEY SALT TO TASTE
- FOR GARNISH
- PARSLEY MINCED,
- CHILI FLAKES
- MELTED BUTTER

18 MINUTES   2 SERVINGS

Instructions:

- Wash and pat dry the beef steak cubes well. Toss the steak cubes and mushrooms in a mixing bowl. Season with Worcestershire sauce, optional garlic powder, and a heavy seasoning of salt and pepper after coating with melted butter.
- Heat the Air Fryer for 4 minutes at 400°F.
- In the air fryer basket, arrange the steak and mushrooms in a uniform layer. Cook the steak and mushrooms for about 10 to18 minutes at 400°F, shaking and rotating twice throughout the air frying procedure (time depends on your preferred doneness, the thickness of the steak, size of the air fryer).
- Examine the steak to check how well done it is. If you want the steak to be more done, grill it for an additional 2-5 minutes.
- Top with parsley and pour some melted butter and/or chili flakes optionally. If needed, season with extra salt and pepper. Serve hot.

Nutritional Values: Calories 401kcal | Protein 32g | Fat 29g | Carbs 3g | Salt 168mg |Sugar 1g |Fibers 1g

JUICY ONION SOUP MIX BURGERS

INGREDIENTS

- 1/2 LB. CHUCK BEEF GROUND
- ½ A PACKET OF ONION SOUP MIX
- TOPPINGS
- HAMBURGER BUNS
- SLICED ONION
- CHEESE
- LETTUCE
- SLICED TOMATO
- MUSTARD
- PICKLES
- KETCHUP

12 MINUTES 2 SERVINGS

Toppings:

- Hamburger Buns
- Sliced Onion
- Cheese
- Lettuce
- Sliced Tomato
- Mustard
- Pickles
- Ketchup

Instructions:

- Mix beef and onion soup in a large mixing bowl and form 4 patties.
- Spray the air fryer basket with olive oil spray after lining it with foil or parchment
- Distribute the patties equally in the basket.

- Cook for 5 minutes at 375°F in the air fryer.
- Cook for a further 5 minutes at 375°F after carefully opening and turning the pan.
- Open the air fryer and check to see whether they are done to your liking or at least 170 degrees.
- If they require more time, increase the cooking time by 2 minutes.
- Serve with chosen garnishes.

Note: If you prefer, you may use pre-made patties and sprinkle the spice on top before cooking

Nutritional Values: Calories 486kcal | Protein 41g | Fat 27g | Carbs 18g | Salt 1279mg |Sugar 4g |Fibers 2g

BAKED MAPLE SALMON

INGREDIENTS

- 1 LB. SALMON FILLETS (ABOUT 2 PIECES), CUT LENGTHWISE INTO 3-INCH
- 1/2 TBSP OLIVE OIL
- 1 TBSP SOY SAUCE
- 1 TSP GARLIC, MINCED
- 1/8 CUP MAPLE SYRUP
- 1/4 TSP GROUND BLACK PEPPER
- 1/2 TBSP ITALIAN SEASONING
- SESAME SEEDS (OPTIONAL, FOR SERVING)

20 MINUTES | 2 SERVINGS

Instructions:

- Stir together olive oil, maple syrup, Italian spice, soy sauce, black pepper, and garlic in a small bowl.
- Drizzle the maple syrup mixture over the salmon fillets in a medium container to coat completely. Marinate for about 30 minutes or overnight in the refrigerator, covered. (Alternatively, marinate the salmon in a big Ziploc bag.)
- After adding all of the ingredients, push the air out of the bag and carefully shut it. To coat the salmon, press the marinade around it.
- Meantime, heat the air fryer at 350 °F. Then, take the seasoned salmon fillets out of the bowl and set them, skin side down, in the basket. Save the marinating sauce for later use.
- Cook at 350 F for 10 minutes, or until cooked thoroughly and flaky. Brush the remaining marinade over the fish halfway through to add more flavor.
- Place the salmon fillets on a platter and set them aside for 5 minutes. Serve warm with steaming rice or creamy mashed potatoes and sesame seeds on top (optional).

Nutritional Values: Calories 392kcal | Protein 51.4g | Fat 14.2g | Carbs 15.8g | Salt 397.2mg | Sugar 12.4g | Fibers 1g

AIR FRIED JUMBO SHRIMP

INGREDIENTS

- 5 LARGE JUMBO SHRIMP, RINSED, DEVEINED, AND PAT DRIED
- 1/2 + 1/4 TBSP SOY SAUCE
- 1/2 TBSP OLIVE OIL
- 1/2 TBSP GARLIC, MINCED
- 1/2 TSP ITALIAN SEASONING
- 1/4 TBSP SUGAR
- 1/2 TSP WHITE SESAME SEEDS FOR GARNISH
- 1/2 TSP GROUND BLACK PEPPER (OPTIONAL)
- 1 TBSP CILANTRO FOR GARNISH

10 MINUTES 2 SERVINGS

For Spicy Mayo Sauce:

- 1 tbsp lime juice
- 1 tbsp Sriracha
- ¼ cup of mayonnaise

Instructions:

- Using scissors, cut through the shrimp shell at the back. Remove the veins, rinse well, and wipe dry with a paper towel.
- Fill a big Ziploc bag halfway with shrimp (or mixing bowl). Mix in all seasonings (soy sauce, olive oil, garlic, sugar, black pepper, and Italian seasoning). Seal the bag and gently massage the shrimp in the marinade to cover. Allow for a 20-minute resting period.
- Fill the air fryer basket halfway with marinated shrimp. Make sure the basket is not too full.
- Air fried the shrimp for 10 minutes at 350°F, or until the crisp and orange shells. Halfway through cooking, shake the basket.

- Place the shrimp on a platter, garnish with cilantro and white sesame seeds and dish out with spicy mayo sauce. To prepare the spicy mayo sauce, whisk together the sriracha, mayonnaise, and lime juice in a small bowl using a spoon.

Nutritional Values: *Calories 107kcal | Protein 10.5g | Fat 5.5g | Carbs 4.8g | Salt 274.1mg |Sugar 2.6g |Fibers 1g*

JUICY GARLIC BUTTER SHRIMP

INGREDIENTS

- 1/2 LB. SHRIMP DEVEINED & PEELED
- 2 TBSP UNSALTED BUTTER
- ½ TSP GARLIC MINCED

8 MINUTES **2 SERVINGS**

Instructions:

- Wash and pat dry the shrimp after removing the shells. Set them aside in a large mixing dish.
- Mix the minced garlic and butter in a small microwave-safe bowl and microwave for thirty seconds, or till the butter is melted.
- Drizzle the butter-garlic mixture all over the shrimp and toss to coat.
- Fill the basket halfway with shrimp, allowing enough space between them, so they do not stack.
- Air fry for 6-10 min at 370 degrees Fahrenheit, stirring halfway through.
- To check for doneness, the bottom of the shrimp tail should be opaque and no longer transparent.

Nutritional Values: Calories 217kcal | Protein 23g | Fat 13g | Carbs 1g | Salt 883mg | Sugar 1g | Fibers 1g

CRAB STUFFED MUSHROOMS

INGREDIENTS

- 1 LB. BABY BELLA MUSHROOMS
- 1 TSP SALT BLEND
- 1 CELERY RIBS, DICED
- 2 TBSP RED ONION, DICED
- 1/4 CUP OF SEASONED BREADCRUMBS
- 4 OZ LUMP CRAB
- 1 SMALL EGG
- 1/4 CUP OF PARMESAN CHEESE, SHREDDED + DIVIDED
- 1/2 TSP HOT SAUCE
- 1/2 TSP OREGANO
- COOKING SPRAY (OLIVE OIL SPRAY PREFERRED)

18 MINUTES   2 SERVINGS

Instructions:

- Preheat the air fryer or the oven to 400°f.
- Cooking spray should be sprayed on the air fryer tray or baking sheet. Mushroom stems should be cut off. Spray the tops of the mushrooms with olive oil cooking spray. To season the mushrooms, sprinkle salt blend on top. Place aside.
- Chop the celery and onion.
- Combine the celery, onions, crab, egg, breadcrumbs, and half of the grated parmesan, spicy and sauce oregano in a mixing bowl.
- Fill the interior of each mushroom and mound it up a little, so it forms a tiny dome.
- Top with the remaining grated parmesan.
- Bake for 8 to 9 minutes in an air fryer. You may need to do many batch runs based on the size of the air fryer

Nutritional Values: Calories 33kcal | Protein 4g | Fat 1g | Carbs 3g| Salt 134mg |Sugar 1g |Fibers 1g

AIR FRIED MAHI MAHI

INGREDIENTS

- 1/2 LB. MAHI-MAHI FILLETS
- 1 TBSP OLIVE OIL
- 1 CUP PANKO BREADCRUMBS
- 1/4 TSP GARLIC POWDER
- 1/2 TSP PAPRIKA
- 1/8 TSP ONION POWDER
- 1/4 TSP PEPPER
- 1/4 TSP SALT
- LEMON WEDGES, FOR SERVING (OPTIONAL)

12 MINUTES   **2 SERVINGS**

Instructions:

- Heat the air fryer to 400°f.
- Drizzle or baste the mahi-mahi fillets with olive oil on a big plate.
- In a shallow dish, combine the panko breadcrumbs, garlic powder, paprika, salt, onion powder, and pepper.
- Cover each Mahi Mahi piece in the panko mixture before placing it in the air fryer basket in a single layer. Spritz with olive oil.
- Cook the Mahi Mahi for 12 to 15 minutes, turning halfway through.
- Take out from the air fryer top with lemon wedges and serve

Nutritional Values: Calories 467kcal | Protein 48g | Fat 11g | Carbs 41g | Salt 853mg | Sugar 4g | Fibers 3g

FALAFEL

INGREDIENTS

- 1/2 + 1/4 CUP DRIED RAW CHICKPEAS, SOAKED OVERNIGHT (DO NOT USE CANNED CHICKPEAS)
- 1/2 SMALL ONION, CHOPPED ROUGHLY
- 1 TSP CUMIN
- 1/4 CUP OF FRESH CILANTRO, CHOPPED
- 2 CLOVES OF GARLIC
- 1/4 CUP OF FRESH PARSLEY, CHOPPED
- 1/4 CUP OF FRESH DILL, CHOPPED
- 1/2 TSP CARDAMOM (OR ITALIAN SEASONING)
- 1/4 CUP TAHINI SAUCE (FOR SERVING)
- 1/4 TSP GROUND BLACK PEPPER
- 1/2 TSP SALT
- 1/2 TBSP ALL-PURPOSE FLOUR (OPTIONAL)
- 1/2 TSP BAKING SODA

15 MINUTES 2 SERVINGS

Instructions:

- Pour the water into a large mixing dish and add the dry chickpeas. Soak them in water overnight (at least 8-10 hours or longer). Ensure that the chickpeas are thoroughly immersed in water at all times.
- Transfer the chickpeas to a food processor after draining them in a colander.
- Combine the onions, parsley, garlic, cilantro, dill, cardamom, cumin, salt, and pepper in a mixing bowl. For roughly 1 minute, pulse on and off until a fine consistency is reached.
- In a large mixing basin, combine the falafel mixture with the flour (optional) and baking soda until equally blended. If the mixture is overly moist, add flour to keep the falafel from coming apart during frying.
- Refrigerate the bowl for about 30 minutes after wrapping it in plastic wrap. This allows the taste to permeate the whole combination.
- To prevent sticking, wet your hands and form the falafel into 1-inch balls with your palms (like meatballs). Alternatively, an ice cream scoop can be used to produce even rounds.

- Heat the air fryer to 376 degrees Fahrenheit for about 3 minutes. Arrange the falafel in the air fryer basket in a single layer and lightly brush with cooking oil to cover evenly. Air cooks the falafel for 12 to14 minutes, or until golden brown. Toss the basket midway while air frying to ensure equal browning.
- Transfer the falafel to a dish. Serve with tahini sauce and a garnish of chopped parsley.

Nutritional Values: *Calories 65kcal | Protein 3.5g | Fat 1g | Carbs 11.2 | Salt 187mg |Sugar 1.8g |Fibers 2g*

VEGETARIAN SPRING ROLLS

INGREDIENTS

- 1 TBSP VEGETABLE OIL
- 1/2 TSP GARLIC, MINCED
- 1/2 TSP GINGER, GRATED
- 1/2 CUP SHIITAKE MUSHROOMS (FRESH OR DRIED*), FINELY CHOPPED
- 1/4 CUP CARROTS, SHREDDED
- 1/2 TBSP GREEN ONIONS, FINELY CHOPPED
- 1 ½ CUPS CABBAGE, SHREDDED
- ¼ TBSP VEGETABLE STOCK POWDER (OPTIONAL)
- 1/2 TBSP SESAME OIL
- 1 TBSP SOY SAUCE
- 1/4 TBSP WHITE PEPPER
- 1 TBSP CORNSTARCH
- 1/2 TSP SUGAR
- 1/2 PACKAGE OF SPRING ROLL WRAPPERS, DEFROSTED OR FRESH (10 PIECES)

8 MINUTES   2 SERVINGS

For the dipping sauce:

- 1 tbsp black vinegar
- ½ tsp green onions, finely sliced
- ½ tsp sriracha (optional)

Instructions:

Prepare the vegetable filling:

- Heat the oil over medium-high heat for 2 minutes in a large skillet. Mix in the garlic, ginger, and mushrooms. Stir for about 1 minute or until aromatic. Mix in the carrots, cabbage, and green onions. Raise the temperature to be high and continue to stir fry for two min.
- Mix the sesame oil, soy sauce, stock powder (if preferred), sugar and white pepper in a bowl. Stir everything together thoroughly, then cover and simmer for 1 minute. (Because cabbage includes a lot of water, the vegetable combination will become soupy.)

- Remove the cover and reduce the heat to medium. Stir in the cornstarch until completely combined. Cornstarch aids in the thickening of the mixture. If necessary, add a little extra. Let the filling cool fully before folding the spring rolls, which should take around 10 to 15 minutes.

Fold the spring rolls:
- On a dry, clean, leveled surface, lay one spring roll wrapper diagonal (diamond shape). To keep the remaining wrappers from drying out, keep them within the packaging.
- Spread up to 1 and 1/2 tbsp of vegetable filling on a 1/2-inch-thick horizontal line, 1/4 inches up from the bottom. On the side corners, leave about 2-inches open.
- Fold the bottom up, so it covers the filling. The bottom corner should be close to the center of the wrapper. Fold the two side corners into the center, then fold over the top.
- Roll the wrapper tightly with your fingers until 1-2 inches remain on top. Brush the remaining top corner lightly with water (or dip your finger into a bowl of water and apply it on the top corner). Roll up tightly to form a burrito. Make certain that all edges are properly sealed.
- Cover with a tea towel and place the top edge side down to keep them from drying out.
- Continue with the leftover spring rolls.
- Spray or brush the spring rolls with oil and arrange them in a single layer in the air fryer basket. Fry in the air fryer at 350°f for 8-10 mins, or until golden and crispy. If you want to acquire that golden tone, brush some additional oil on them halfway through. It will not be as brown as deep-frying, but it will be healthier because you will be using much less oil.
- Rep with the leftover spring rolls.

  To make the vinegar dipping sauce

- Combine the black vinegar, sriracha (if used), and green onions in a small bowl. With a spoon, mix everything.
- Serve with the spring rolls as a dipping sauce.ù

Nutritional Values: Calories 65kcal | Protein 1.7g | Fat 1.9g | Carbs 10.4g | Salt 120.5mg |Sugar 0.9g |Fibers

VEGAN AIR FRIED RAVIOLI

INGREDIENTS

- ¼ CUP OF PANKO BREADCRUMBS
- 1/2 TSP OREGANO DRIED
- 1 TSP OF NUTRITIONAL YEAST FLAKES
- 1/2 TSP BASIL DRIED
- 1/8 CUP OF AQUAFABA LIQUID FROM A CAN OF CHICKPEAS
- 1/2 TSP GARLIC POWDER
- 4 OZ THAWED OR FROZEN VEGAN RAVIOLI
- 1/4 CUP MARINARA FOR DIPPING
- PINCH PEPPER & SALT
- SPRITZ COOKING SPRAY

8 MINUTES **2 SERVINGS**

Instructions:

- Mix the panko breadcrumbs, garlic powder, dried basil, nutritional yeast flakes, dried oregano, salt, and pepper in a dish.
- Place aquafaba in another small bowl
- Coat ravioli in bread crumb mixture after dipping in aquafaba and shaking off excess liquid. Ensure the ravioli is completely coated. Place the ravioli in an air fryer basket. Continue breading the ravioli until all of them are breaded. To ensure that the ravioli brown evenly, does not overcrowd them in the air fryer. (Air fry in batches as required.)
- Spray the ravioli in cooking spray.
- Preheat the air fryer to 390°f. 6 minutes in the air fryer, flip each ravioli carefully. (Do not just jiggle the basket. You will lose a lot of breadcrumbs if you do.) 2 minutes longer in the air fryer.
- Remove the ravioli from the air fryer and dish out with warm marinara as a dipping sauce.

Nutritional Values: *Calories 150kcal | Protein 5g | Fat 0g | Carbs 27g | Salt 411mg |Sugar 1g |Fibers 2g*

POPCORN TOFU

INGREDIENTS

- 7 OZ (IN WATER) EXTRA-FIRM TOFU, DRAINED & PRESSED
- 1/4 CUP OF QUINOA FLOUR
- 1 TBSP NUTRITIONAL YEAST
- 1/4 CUP OF CORNMEAL
- 1 TSP GARLIC POWDER
- 1 TBSP VEGETARIAN BOUILLON
- 1/2 TBSP DIJON MUSTARD
- 1/4 TSP SALT
- 1 TSP ONION POWDER
- 1/4 TSP PEPPER
- 3/4 CUP OF PANKO BREADCRUMBS
- 1/2 CUP OF DAIRY-FREE MILK UNSWEETENED MORE IF NEEDED

12 MINUTES 2 SERVINGS

For Sriracha Mayo:

- 1/4 cup of vegan mayo
- 1 tbsp sriracha

Instructions:

- Cut the pressed tofu into chew-size chunks.
- In a large mixing bowl, combine the flour, cornmeal, nutritional yeast, better than bouillon, mustard, garlic, onion, salt, pepper, and milk. The thickness should be similar to that of pancake batter. If necessary, add additional milk to thin it down.
- In a separate dish, combine the panko breadcrumbs.
- Put in as many nuggets as will fit in the air fryer basket. You do not want the basket to be too packed or stay together, so do it in batches. Preheat the air fryer to 350°F for 12 minutes. Shake the basket once. Serve with popcorn tofu and a mixture of sriracha and vegan mayo.

Nutritional Values: Calories 261kcal | Protein 16g | Fat 6g | Carbs 37.5g | Salt 548mg |Sugar 2.4g |Fibers 4.8g

VEGAN CRUNCH WRAP

INGREDIENTS

- 2 TBSP PINTO BEANS REFRIED
- 1 GLUTEN-FREE TORTILLA REGULAR SIZE
- 1 SMALL CORN TORTILLA
- 2 TBSP VEGAN CHEESE GRATED OR QUESO SAUCE
- 2-3 ICEBERG LETTUCE LEAVES
- 2-3 TBSP SALSA
- 2 TBSP SLICED AVOCADO OR GUACAMOLE

8 MINUTES | 2 SERVINGS

Instructions:

- Preheat the air fryer to 325 degrees Fahrenheit
- Arrange each crunch wrap by layering them in the following order:
    1. A large normal tortilla
    2. Meat or beans
    3. Cheese sauce or grated cheese
    4. Corn tortilla, small
    5. Salsa
    6. Iceberg lettuce leaves in their whole
    7. Avocado slices or guacamole
- Heat the Taco Crunch Wrap in the air fryer for 6 minutes at 350°F.
- Bake for 5-8 minutes, or until warmed through and slightly crispy, at 325°F. For dipping, serve with dairy-free sour cream and guacamole.

Nutritional Values: Calories 519kcal | Protein 22g | Fat 27g | Carbs 43g | Salt 430mg | Sugar 9g | Fibers 26g

BAKED APPLE CHIPS

INGREDIENTS
- 2 GALA APPLES

20 MINUTES 2 SERVINGS

Instructions:

- Slice the apples into extremely thin slices, about 1/8 thick, starting from the base. To slice, use a mandolin or a knife.
- Put them in a single, equal layer on the air fryer basket. There is no need to space between the apple slices because they will decrease. Sprinkle some cinnamon on top for added flavor.
- Preheat the air fryer for 3 minutes at 200 degrees Fahrenheit. Place apple slices in an air fryer basket in a single layer and air-fried for 20 minutes, or until crispy.

Nutritional Values: Calories 71kcal | Protein 0.4g | Fat 0.2g | Carbs 18.9g Salt 1.4mg |Sugar 14.2g |Fibers 5g

AIR FRYER TATER TOTS

INGREDIENTS
- 8 OZ POTATO TOTS

15 MINUTES | 2 SERVINGS

Instructions:

- Heat the Air Fryer to 400 degrees F.
- Prepare the liner of the basket with olive oil spray or parchment paper.
- Place the tater tots in a single layer in the basket of the Air Fryer.
- Cook for 15 minutes at 400 degrees Fahrenheit, turning every 5 minutes. For extra crunchy tots, cook in one-minute intervals.

Nutritional Values: Calories 201kcal | Protein 2g | Fat 9g | Carbs 29g | Salt 485mg | Sugar 1g | Fibers 2g

CANDIED WALNUTS

INGREDIENTS

- 1 TBSP BUTTER MELTED UNSALTED
- 1 TSP VANILLA EXTRACT
- 2 CUPS OF WALNUTS HALVED
- 1 TBSP BROWN SUGAR
- 1/4 TSP SALT
- 1/2 TBSP SUGAR
- 1/4 TSP CINNAMON

10 MINUTES   2 SERVINGS

Instructions

- Heat the air fryer to 200°F.
- While the air fryer is heating up, prep the walnuts by tossing them in a medium mixing dish with the melted butter and vanilla extract.
- Mix the walnuts till they are soaked with the butter and vanilla, allowing the rest of the ingredients to adhere to them.
- After the walnuts have been coated, whisk in the brown sugar, sugar, cinnamon, and salt. Stir the walnuts with the remaining ingredients to coat evenly.
- Finally, place them in the air fryer basket and cook for 10 minutes at 200 °F, tossing or shaking the basket halfway through.

Nutritional Values: Calories 217kcal | Protein 4g | Fat 20g | Carbs 7g | Salt 74mg | Sugar 4g | Fibers 2g

LOW CARB AIR FRIED ONION RINGS

INGREDIENTS

- 1/2 ONION SLICED
- ½ CUP FLOUR
- 1/2 EGG BEATEN
- 1/2 TSP BAKING POWDER
- 1/2 CUP + 1 TSP MILK
- 1/2 CUP BREADCRUMBS SEASONINGS

16 MINUTES   2 SERVINGS

Instructions:

- Heat the air fryer to 370°f and prepare a non-stick basket. Combine the flour, baking powder, and spices in a mixing basin. Mix in the egg, followed by the milk (or beer). Place in a small dish. Place the breadcrumbs in a small basin. Using a fork, totally cover the slice of onion with the ingredients of the first bowl, using a dipping technique. Then roll this in the breadcrumbs. After that, put it in the basket. Continue with the remaining slices, being careful not to overlap them too much.
- Cook the onion rings for 8 minutes before flipping them. Continue to air fry for 8 minutes more, or until done.

Nutritional Values: Calories 172kcal | Protein 11g | Fat 4g | Carbs 15g | Salt 989mg | Sugar 7g | Fibers 1g

AIR FRIED MACARONI&CHEESE BALL

INGREDIENTS

- 2 CUPS MACARONI AND CHEESE LEFTOVER
- 1 TBSP MILK
- 1 EGG
- 1/2 CUP OF JAPANESE PANKO
- 1/2 TSP SALT
- 1/4 TSP GARLIC POWDER
- 1/2 TSP PAPRIKA
- 1 SLICE OF COOKED BACON FINELY CHOPPED (OPTIONAL)

8 MINUTES　2 SERVINGS

Instructions:

- Take big portions of leftover refrigerated macaroni and cheese, about 2 tbsp, and shape into balls. Place aside.
- Whisk together the egg and milk in a mixing bowl. Then, in a separate bowl, mix the panko breadcrumbs, garlic powder, salt, diced bacon and paprika, if using.
- Place a macaroni and cheese ball in the egg and milk mixture, coating the entire ball, then in the panko mixture, and finally on a baking sheet fitted with parchment paper. Place the container in the freezer for 30 minutes.
- Heat the air fryer to 360°f. After 30 minutes, take the mac and cheese balls from the freezer and arrange them in a single layer inside the air fryer basket, ensuring they do not touch. Cook for 8-10 mins, or till the exterior is crisp and golden. Take out, serve, and enjoy.

Nutritional Values: Calories 887kcal | Protein 37g | Fat 30g | Carbs 116g | Salt 2539mg |Sugar 1g |Fibers 1g

AIR FRIED BUTTERNUT SQUASH

INGREDIENTS

- 2 CUPS (ABOUT 1/4 MED-SIZED) BUTTERNUT SQUASH, ½-INCH CUBES
- 1/2 TSP ITALIAN SEASONING
- 1 TBSP OLIVE OIL
- 1/2 TSP GARLIC POWDER
- 1/8 TSP GROUND BLACK PEPPER
- 1/4 TSP SALT
- PUMPKIN SEEDS (, FOR SERVING OPTIONAL)

15 MINUTES — 2 SERVINGS

Instructions:

- Place all ingredients in a large bowl, including the butternut squash, Italian seasoning, olive oil, garlic powder, pepper, and salt. To mix, toss everything together.
- Transfer to the air fryer basket and put in a single layer. You may need to do this in two batches, based on the size of the air fryer. Cook for 12 to 15 minutes at 400°f, or until crisp and crunchy.
- Finish with a sprinkling of pumpkin seeds.

Nutritional Values: Calories 308kcal | Protein 11.4g | Fat 23g | Carbs 20.9g | Salt 299.3mg | Sugar 3.6g | Fibers 6g

ROASTED GARLIC GREEN BEANS

INGREDIENTS

- 1/2 LB. GREEN BEANS, WASHED AND TRIMMED
- 1/2 TSP SESAME OIL
- 1/2 TBSP VEGETABLE OIL
- 1/2 TBSP GARLIC, MINCED
- 1/2 TSP ITALIAN SEASONING
- 1/2 TSP BALSAMIC VINEGAR
- 1/2 TSP WORCESTERSHIRE SAUCE
- 1/4 TSP BLACK PEPPER (OR TO TASTE)
- 1/2 TSP SOY SAUCE

10 MINUTES 2 SERVINGS

Instructions:

- Heat the air fryer at 350 F.
- Green beans should be washed and trimmed before being dried with a paper towel. Combine them in a large bowl with the remaining ingredients. To mix, toss everything together.
- Cook in the air fryer: place the green beans in the air fryer basket and cook for 10 minutes at 350 f, or until cooked but still crisp. Halfway through cooking, shake the basket.

Nutritional Values: Calories 83kcal | Protein 2.4g | Fat 4.8g | Carbs 9.8g | Salt 57.7mg | Sugar 4.1g | Fibers 8g

CRISPY AIR FRIED FRENCH FRIES

INGREDIENTS

- 1 MED-SIZES RUSSET POTATOES, WASHED
- 1/2 TBSP OLIVE OIL
- 1/8 TSP GARLIC POWDER (OPTIONAL)
- 1/8 TSP SALT
- PINCH OF BLACK PEPPER, TO TASTE
- FLAKED SEA SALT, FOR SERVING

12 MINUTES 2 SERVINGS

Instructions:

- Heat the air fryer to 375 degrees Fahrenheit for 5 minutes
- Cut the potatoes into long, 1/4-inch-thick strips (French fry form).
- Place the sliced potatoes in a large bowl and toss with olive oil, garlic powder (optional), salt, and pepper. To coat, toss everything together.
- Cook for 12 to 13 minutes, until crispy and golden, in an air fryer basket with a single layer of potatoes. If the potatoes overlap, they will not cook evenly or crisply.
- Serve hot with sea salt flakes on top, and ketchup, spicy mayo, or other dipping sauce on the side.

Nutritional Values: Calories 115kcal | Protein 2.3g | Fat 3.6g | Carbs 19.4g | Salt 150.8mg | Sugar 0.7g | Fibers 5g

2-INGREDIENT DOUGH BAGELS

INGREDIENTS

- 1/3 CUP OF SELF-RISING FLOUR
- 1/3 CUP OF NON-FAT GREEK YOGURT
- 1/3 OF EGG, FOR WASH
- OPTIONAL TOPPINGS:
- 1 TSP EVERYTHING BUT THE BAGEL SEASONING

10 MINUTES   2 SERVINGS

Instructions:

- In a big mixing bowl, mix 1 cup self-rising flour and 1 cup yogurt. Stir with a rubber spatula or wooden spoon until the mixture thickens and forms a dough ball.
- Lay the dough on a well-floured board and cut it into 4 or 6 equal pieces. Sprinkle a little additional flour on the table to keep the dough sticking.
- Roll each wedge of dough into a short rope approximately 6-8 inches long to make bagels. Join the ends of each piece to form a bagel-shaped circular.
- In a mixing bowl, beat the egg, and then brush the egg wash on the bagels using a pastry brush.
- Before you cook the bagel, sprinkle it with any desired toppings. After that, put the bagels in the air fryer basket.
- Cook the bagels for about 10 minutes in an air fryer at 350 degrees f. When the bagels are done, they will start to become golden brown.

Nutritional Values: Calories 107kcal | Protein 7g | Fat 1g | Carbs | Salt 156mg |Sugar 1g |Fibers 1g

CRISPY POTATO WEDGES

INGREDIENTS

- 1 MEDIUM-SIZED RUSSET POTATOES, SLICE INTO WEDGES
- 1/2 TBSP OLIVE OIL
- 1/8 TSP GARLIC POWDER
- 1/4 TSP PAPRIKA
- A PINCH OF CAYENNE PEPPER
- 1/8 TSP GROUND BLACK PEPPER
- 1/2 TSP SEA SALT

TO SERVE (OPTIONAL):

- 1/4 CUP OF PARMESAN CHEESE GRATED
- 1/2 TBSP PARSLEY CHOPPED

15 MINUTES   2 SERVINGS

Instructions:

- Put raw potato wedges in cold water and 2 cups of ice cubes in a dish. Allow them to soak for at least 30 minutes before draining and patting dry with paper towels.
- If your model calls for it, preheat the Air Fryer.
- Mix olive oil, garlic powder, paprika, cayenne pepper, black pepper, and salt in a big mixing bowl or Ziplock bag. Toss in the potato wedges to coat them with spice.
- Place the wedges in the air fryer basket and cook for 15 minutes at 400F. (200C). Every 5 minutes, shake the basket. Depending on the size of your Air Fryer, you may have to cook them in batches.
- In a mixing dish, add the grated Parmesan cheese and, if using, the parsley. Toss the cooked wedges in the bowl with the topping until evenly covered. On the side, serve with sour cream or ketchup

Nutritional Values: Calories 187kcal | Protein 7g | Fat 9g | Carbs 20g | Salt 779mg | Sugar 1g | Fibers 1g

EASY BLUEBERRY MUFFIN BITES

INGREDIENTS

- ½ CUP ALL-PURPOSE FLOUR
- ¼ TSP CINNAMON
- 1 ½ TBSP SUGAR
- 1/6 CUP OF MILK
- 1/8 CUP OF BUTTER, UNSALTED MELTED (HALF A STICK)
- 1/2 TSP VANILLA
- 1/2 AN EGG
- ¼ CUP OF FROZEN OR FRESH BLUEBERRIES

6 MINUTES   2 SERVINGS

Instructions:

- In a large dish, mix the flour, cinnamon, and sugar.
- Add in the egg, milk, vanilla extract, and melted butter. Stir all together with a fork till it is fully incorporated.
- Fold the blueberries into the batter gently until they are equally distributed.
- Pour an ice cream scoop into the silicone cups approximately a quarter of the way. Fill paper muffin liners 3/4 full if using a small muffin tray.
- Place gently into the basket. Air fry for 4-6 minutes 350°F.

Nutritional Values: Calories 295kcal | Protein 6g | Fat 14g | Carbs 37g | Salt 29mg | Sugar 12g | Fibers 1g

HONEY GLAZED PEARS

INGREDIENTS

- 2 SMALL PEARS
- 1 TBSP BROWN SUGAR
- 1 ½ TBSP BUTTER, MELTED
- 1 TSP CINNAMON
- 1 TBSP HONEY
- ½ A SHEET OF FROZEN PUFF PASTRY

10 MINUTES **2 SERVINGS**

Instructions:

- Set aside after coring each pear, keeping the stem on the top. (If you are going to cut the pear into slices, you do not need to core it first.)
- Combine the honey, melted butter, cinnamon, and brown sugar in a medium mixing. Bowl and spoon over each pear individually with the mixture.
- Puff pastry sheets may be cut into strips ranging from 1/2 to 3/4 inches wide. Wrap the pastry strip around the pear till it is completely wrapped, beginning at the top.
- Brush the pears with another light layer of the honey mixture.
- Air fries the pears in the air fryer for about 8 to 10 minutes at 360°f, or until
- Serve with ice cream or cool whip.

Nutritional Values: Calories 554kcal | Protein 5g | Fat 32g | Carbs 66g | Salt 231mg | Sugar 29g | Fibers 6g

NUTELLA FRENCH TOAST ROLL-UPS

INGREDIENTS

- 5 TSP NUTELLA
- 5 SLICES OF BREAD
- 1 LARGE EGG
- 2 TBSP GRANULATED WHITE SUGAR
- 1/2 TSP CINNAMON
- 1 TBSP MILK

6 MINUTES | 2 SERVINGS

Instructions:

- If you have not done so, let the bread out to stale for 30 minutes to an hour.
- You may put the bread out longer if you prepare beforehand.
- Set aside the eggs and milk that have been whisked together.
- Set aside the cinnamon and sugar on a small dish.
- Remove the crusts from the bread pieces and flatten them with a glass or rolling pin.
- Spread a spoonful of Nutella on one end of the deflated bread. Curl the bread up and smear a little Nutella on the tip to help keep it closed and tight during cooking.
- Immerse the French toast rolls in the beaten egg mixture before rolling them in the sugar and cinnamon mixture.
- Arrange the Nutella- filled French Toast Rolls-ups in the air fryer basket that has been preheated. Cook for 5-6 minutes at 360°F, turning the roll-ups halfway through.
- Serve right away.

Nutritional Values: Calories 362kcal | Protein 13g | Fat 10g | Carbs 55g | Salt 425mg | Sugar 23g | Fibers 4g

QUICK BROWNIES

INGREDIENTS

FOR WET INGREDIENTS
- 1/8 CUP OF NON-DAIRY MILK
- 1/8 CUP OF AQUAFABA
- 1/4 TSP VANILLA EXTRACT

FOR DRY INGREDIENTS
- 1/4 CUP OF WHOLE WHEAT PASTRY FLOUR
- ½ TBSP GROUND FLAX SEEDS
- ¼ CUP OF VEGAN SUGAR
- 1/8 CUP OF COCOA POWDER
- 1/8 TSP SALT

ADD-INS
- 1/8 CUP OF ANYONE OR A MIX OF THE FOLLOWING:
- CHOPPED HAZELNUTS, WALNUTS, PECANS, SHREDDED COCONUT, MINI VEGAN CHOCOLATE CHIPS

20 MINUTES 2 SERVINGS

Instructions:

- In a separate dish, combine the dry ingredients. Then, in a large measuring cup, combine the wet ingredients. Mix the wet and dry ingredients well.
- Mix in the add-in(s) of your choosing.
- Heat the air fryer to 350°f (or as close as your air fryer gets). To keep it fully oil-free, spray a 5-inch round pie pan or cake pan (or a loaf pan that can fit in the air fryer) with oil or cover it with butter paper.
- Insert the pan into the frying basket. The cooking time is 20 minutes. If the center is not well set or a knife inserted into the center does not come out clean, cook for 5 minutes longer and repeat as needed. The time will vary depending on the size of the pan and your air fryer.

Nutritional Values: Calories 225.3kcal | Protein 4g | Fat 6.8g | Carbs 41g | Salt 157.8mg |Sugar 25g |Fibers 4.8g

PLAIN CAKE

INGREDIENTS

- 1 CUP OF GRANULATED SUGAR
- ¾ CUP + 2 TBSP OF ALL-PURPOSE FLOUR
- ½ CUP OF COCOA POWDER UNSWEETENED
- ½ TSP KOSHER SALT
- 1 TSP BAKING POWDER
- 1 LARGE EGG
- ½ TSP BAKING SODA
- ¼ CUP OF VEGETABLE OIL
- ½ CUP OF BUTTERMILK
- ½ CUP OF BOILING WATER
- 1 TSP OF VANILLA EXTRACT

25 MINUTES 2 SERVINGS

Instructions:

- Heat the air fryer to 350 °F.
- Coat the interior of a 7-inch air fryer-safe cake pan with baking spray, then line with a 9-inch circular piece of parchment paper, allowing it to drape up the edges slightly. Set aside and spray with extra cooking spray.
- Stir together the flour, sugar, baking soda, cocoa powder, salt, and baking powder in a large mixing bowl. Combine the buttermilk, egg, vanilla extract, and vegetable oil into the mixing bowl. Blend for 2 minutes, or till thoroughly incorporated. To make a thin batter, stir in hot water.
- Put the batter in the air fryer basket after pouring it into the prepared pan.
- Put in the air fryer for 25 mins, or till the cake is completely done and a toothpick put into it comes out clean. Cool for 10 minutes in the pan before transferring to a wire rack to cool fully.
- If desired, decorate with sprinkles and frosting

Nutritional Values: Calories 269kcal | Protein 3g | Fat 11g | Carbs 41g | Salt 343mg | Sugar 34g | Fibers 1g

4 WEEKS MEAL PLAN

WEEK	BREAKFAST	LUNCH	SNACK	DINNER
1 WEEK	Nutella French Toast Roll-Ups	Sweet Chili Bites	Baked Apple Chips	Air Fryer Mongolian Beef
2 WEEK	Hash Browns	Cheesy Buffalo Cauliflower Bites	Candied Walnuts	Pork Roast
3 WEEK	Popcorn Tofu	Crunch Wrap	Falafel	Juicy Turkey Burgers
4 WEEK	Honey Glazed Pears	Juicy Turkey Burgers	Low Carb Air Fried Onion Rings	Vegan Air Fried Raviol

Conclusion

While many of the greatest air-fryer recipes are for deep-fried items, this gadget may also be used to bake vegetables, roast meat, and bake cookies.

Homemade Finger Foods

If you want to cook your finger foods from scratch, the air fryer is an excellent choice for crisp handmade snacks and sides—try Air-Fryer Potato Wedges, Air-Fryer Tater Tots, Or Air-Fryer Popcorn Tofu.

While air-fried frozen mozzarella sticks are delectable, fresh cheese melts into a mushy mass (so homemade cheese curds are out).

Finger Foods

When it comes to making frozen items designed to taste deep-fried, the air fryer shines. Frozen French fries, mozzarella sticks, and chicken nuggets are a few examples of the various frozen air-fried delicacies available.

Roasted Vegetable

Because air fryers are basically miniature conventional ovens, they are ideal for roasting vegetables, particularly if you are just preparing for one or two people. Air-Fryer Cabbage Steaks and Air-Fryer Hash Browns are a couple of our favorite air-fryer veggie dishes.

However, if you use this gadget to prepare vegetables, leave off the leafy greens.

Meat, chicken, and fish

You can prepare a delicate and juicy air fryer chicken. Air-fryer chicken dishes, such as Air-Fryer Hot Chicken Breasts, are worth a try. Air-Fryer Keto Meatballs are a terrific alternative for a healthier option. Air-Fryer Jumbo Garlic Shrimps is one of our favorite fish and seafood meals.

Some Baked Goods

Air fryers are ideal for producing single-serving sweets such as cookies and apple fritters. Make brownies for the winter holidays or Air-Fryer Nutella French toast roll-ups for a delicious treat any time of year. You cannot, however, make anything that requires a liquid batter.

Printed in Great Britain
by Amazon